THE SCIENCE BEHIND TRACK AND FIELD

by Jenny Fretland VanVoorst

pogo

Ideas for Parents and Teachers

Pogo Books let children practice reading informational text while introducing them to nonfiction features such as headings, labels, sidebars, maps, and diagrams, as well as a table of contents, glossary, and index.

Carefully leveled text with a strong photo match offers early fluent readers the support they need to succeed.

Before Reading

• "Walk" through the book and point out the various nonfiction features. Ask the student what purpose each feature serves.

• Look at the glossary together. Read and discuss the words.

Read the Book

• Have the child read the book independently.

• Invite him or her to list questions that arise from reading.

After Reading

• Discuss the child's questions. Talk about how he or she might find answers to those questions.

• Prompt the child to think more. Ask: Track and field has running, jumping, and throwing events. How are these similar to your favorite field day events?

Pogo Books are published by Jump!
5357 Penn Avenue South
Minneapolis, MN 55419
www.jumplibrary.com

Library of Congress Cataloging-in-Publication Data

Names: Fretland VanVoorst, Jenny, 1972- author.
Title: The science behind track and field / by Jenny Fretland VanVoorst.
Description: Pogo Books Edition. | Minneapolis, Minnesota: Jump!, Inc., [2020] | Series: STEM in the Summer Olympics | Audience: Ages: 7-10. Includes bibliographical references and index.
Identifiers: LCCN 2019004543 (print)
LCCN 2019009715 (ebook)
ISBN 9781641289139 (ebook)
ISBN 9781641289115 (hardcover: alk. paper)
Subjects: LCSH: Track and field—Juvenile literature. Sports sciences—Juvenile literature. Olympics—Juvenile literature.
Classification: LCC GV557 (ebook)
LCC GV557 .F74 2020 (print) | DDC 796.42–dc23
LC record available at https://lccn.loc.gov/2019004543

Editor: Susanne Bushman
Designer: Michelle Sonnek

Photo Credits: Africa Studio/Shutterstock, cover (clipboard); Elnur/Shutterstock, cover (shoes); PA Images/Alamy, 1, 8-9, 13; AWelshLad/iStock, 3 (top); wavebreakmedia/Shutterstock, 3 (middle), 23 (left); John_Kasawa/iStock, 3 (bottom); KAI PFAFFENBACH/REUTERS/Newscom, 4; OLIVIER MORIN/AFP/Getty, 5; ANTONIN THUILLIER/AFP/Getty, 6-7; FABRICE COFFRINI/AFP/Getty, 10-11; FRANCK FIFE/AFP/Getty, 12, 19; JOHANNES EISELE/AFP/Getty, 14-15; JEWEL SAMAD/AFP/Getty, 16-17; CP DC Press/Shutterstock, 18; ADRIAN DENNIS/AFP/Getty, 20-21; amriphoto/iStock, 23 (right).

Printed in the United States of America at Corporate Graphics in North Mankato, Minnesota.

TABLE OF CONTENTS

CHAPTER 1

RACE FOR GOLD

Some track and field Olympians jump. Others throw.

javelin · · · · ·▶

These Olympians race over hurdles. Track and field is made up of many events. The best athletes use **physics** to go for gold!

On your marks! Get set! Go! Many track and field events involve running. Olympic runners have to think about **forces**. **Thrust** is a force runners create. They use their muscles! It moves them forward. They want to be **aerodynamic**.

DID YOU KNOW?

The marathon is the longest Olympic race. It is 26.2 miles (42.195 kilometers) long. That is more than the length of 384 football fields!

Drag works against thrust. It happens as runners move. It is caused by the **friction** of air. They wear tight clothes. They keep their hair back. Why? Air can catch on these and create drag.

Gravity is another force runners face. But Olympians use it to help. How? They lean forward slightly as they run. Gravity pulls them forward. They can move faster with less effort.

DID YOU KNOW?

Who is the fastest person on Earth? As of 2019, **sprinter** Usain Bolt held the record. He ran 100 meters (328 feet) in 9.58 seconds! Will someone run faster at the next Olympics?

CHAPTER 2

JUMP HIGH AND FAR

In some events, such as the high jump and pole vault, athletes need to jump high.

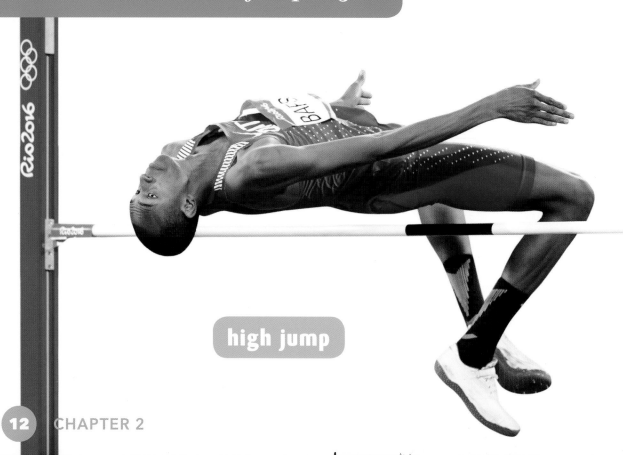

high jump

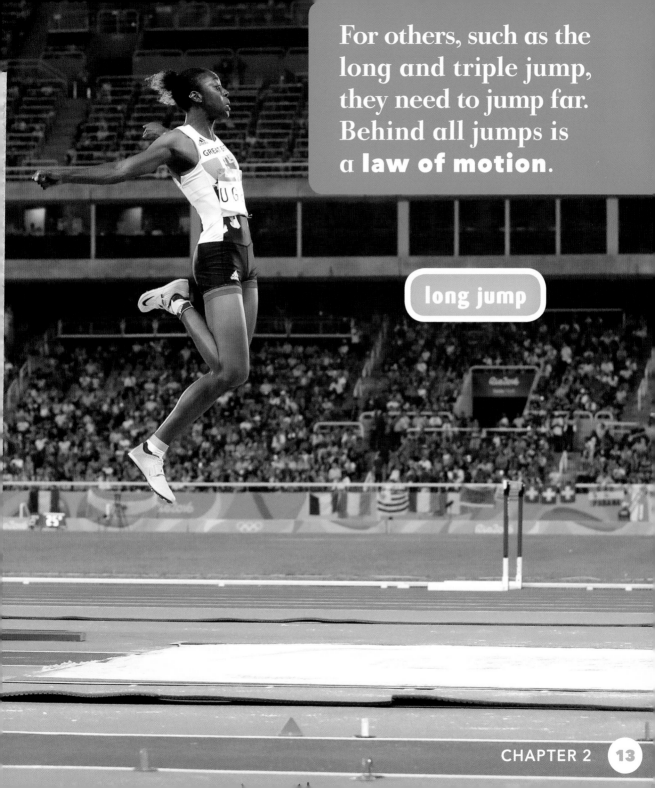

For others, such as the long and triple jump, they need to jump far. Behind all jumps is a **law of motion**.

long jump

What is this law? Every action has an equal and opposite reaction. What does this mean?

When you jump, you push off from the ground. This applies force to the ground. The ground returns your downward force with the same strength. What is the result? You spring up! If you push harder, you jump higher.

DID YOU KNOW?

This law applies to running, too! A sprinter pushes off from starting blocks. The blocks return the push in the direction the runner is going.

Pole vaulters use science, too. The vaulter runs. **Kinetic energy** builds up. This is the energy of motion. Greater speed creates greater kinetic energy.

She jumps! The pole turns the kinetic energy into **potential energy**. This energy comes from location. More kinetic energy creates more potential energy.

TAKE A LOOK!

What gives a pole vaulter kinetic and potential energy?
Take a look!

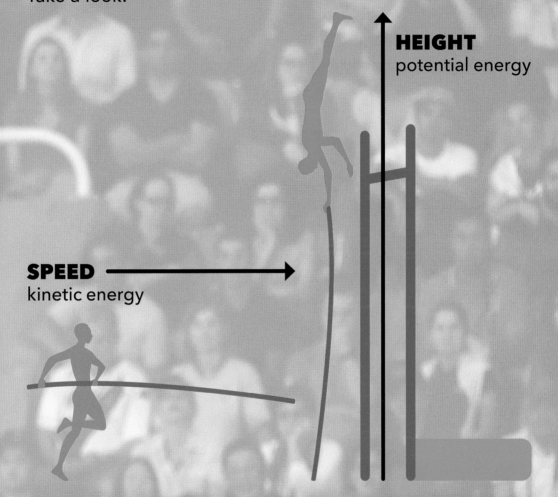

HEIGHT
potential energy

SPEED
kinetic energy

CHAPTER 3

WIND UP AND THROW

Shot put is a throwing event. These athletes throw a heavy ball. How far can they throw?

Hammer throw is another. A ball on a wire is launched down the field.

discus

Some throwing events use a windup. In discus, the thrower spins around. His body twists. This builds up a force called **torque**. Torque provides extra power to the throw. The athlete stops moving. He releases the discus. All of his energy transfers to the object. Zoom! The discus sails into the air.

Olympic stars use science to take home medals! How can you use science during your next field day?

ACTIVITIES & TOOLS

NOODLE JAVELIN

Use a pool noodle as a javelin!
Can you use science to throw farther?

What You Need:
- a pool noodle
- items to mark your landing spots

❶ Stand and hold the center of the pool noodle.

❷ Throw the noodle as hard and as far as you can. Mark the spot where it lands. This is your baseline.

❸ Now think about how Olympic athletes increase their forces. How can you apply what you've learned to improve your throw? You might try using the ground's reaction force by jumping while you throw. You could spin around to increase torque and then throw. You could build up kinetic energy by running into the throw.

❹ After each throw, mark the landing spot. Try each technique three times. Then take a look at your results. Did any of the techniques help you throw farther? If so, why do you think that is? And if not, why not?

GLOSSARY

aerodynamic: Designed to move through the air very easily and quickly.

drag: The force that slows or blocks motion or advancement.

forces: Actions that produce, stop, or change the shape of movements or objects.

friction: The force that slows objects when they rub against each other.

gravity: The force that pulls things toward the center of Earth and keeps them from floating away.

kinetic energy: The energy of motion.

law of motion: One of the three laws of physics that govern moving objects, such as every action has an equal and opposite reaction, that was discovered by Isaac Newton.

physics: The science that deals with matter, energy, and their interactions.

potential energy: Stored energy that can be released to turn into kinetic energy.

sprinter: An athlete who specializes in running short distances at high speeds.

thrust: The force that drives a person or object forward.

torque: The force created by twisting or turning.

INDEX

TO LEARN MORE

Finding more information is as easy as 1, 2, 3.

❶ Go to www.factsurfer.com

❷ Enter "sciencebehindtrackandfield" into the search box.

❸ Choose your book to see a list of websites.

FACT SURFER